new inspirations in
WEDDING FLORALS

TERRY L. RYE

BETTERWAY BOOKS
CINCINNATI, OHIO

metric conversion chart

TO CONVERT	TO	MULTIPLY BY
Inches	Centimeters	2.54
Centimeters	Inches	0.4
Feet	Centimeters	30.5
Centimeters	Feet	0.03
Yards	Meters	0.9
Meters	Yards	1.1
Sq. Inches	Sq. Centimeters	6.45
Sq. Centimeters	Sq. Inches	0.16
Sq. Feet	Sq. Meters	0.09
Sq. Meters	Sq. Feet	10.8
Sq. Yards	Sq. Meters	0.8
Sq. Meters	Sq. Yards	1.2
Pounds	Kilograms	0.45
Kilograms	Pounds	2.2
Ounces	Grams	28.4
Grams	Ounces	0.04

New Inspirations in Wedding Florals. © 2003 by Terry L. Rye. Manufactured in China. All rights reserved. It is permissible for the purchaser to make the projects contained herein and sell them at fairs, bazaars and craft shows. No other part of this book may be reproduced in any form or by any electronic or mechanical means including information storage and retrieval systems without permission in writing from the publisher, except by a reviewer, who may quote a brief passage in review. Published by Betterway Books, an imprint of F&W Publications, Inc., 4700 East Galbraith Road, Cincinnati, Ohio 45236. (800) 289-0963. First edition.

07 06 05 04 03   5 4 3 2 1

Library of Congress Cataloging-in-Publication Data
Rye, Terry L., 1955-
  New inspirations in wedding florals / Terry L. Rye.
      p. cm.
  ISBN 1-55870-634-8 (pbk. : alk. paper)
  1. Wedding decorations. 2. Floral decorations. 3. Bridal bouquets. I. Title.
  SB449.5.W4R95 2003
  745.92'6--dc21

                                   2003051155

Editor: Krista Hamilton and Catherine Cochran
Designer: Stephanie Strang
Layout Artist: Matthew De Rhodes
Production Coordinator: Sara Dumford
Photographer: Christine Polomsky and Al Parrish
Photo Stylist: Jan Nickum

about THE AUTHOR

TERRY RYE'S passion for flowers has allowed her to have the best job in the world—creating innovative and beautiful floral designs. Since 1980, she has been the owner of the Mariemont Florist in Cincinnati, Ohio. The Mariemont Florist has been featured in the prestigious Cincinnati Flower Show and is regarded as a distinguished Professional Florist. As a self-taught floral designer, Terry loves to share the joy of floral arranging with others through her series of how-to books. She has appeared on the DIY Network, part of the HGTV family, as well as having been featured in various national trade publications. Terry resides in Cincinnati with her nine-year-old daughter, Sarah.

dedication

With love and appreciation, I dedicate this book to my dear husband, Doug Eisele, for always being there for me. I am so grateful for his guidance, support and continuous encouragement.

✦

acknowledgments

many thanks to all the talented people in my business, The Mariemont Florist, for their support and dedication during the completion of this book and for their contributions.

Many thanks to my editor, Catherine Cochran, for her meticulous note-taking throughout the step-by-step process and her creative input in making this a truly a special how-to book for wedding florals. Thanks also to Christine Polomsky for her exceptional photography and ability to conceptualize photos that are clear and easy to understand. Many heartfelt thanks always go to Tricia Waddell who has helped make these wonderful books possible.

I am truly blessed with a talented staff, great publisher, wonderful friends and an incredibly supportive, loving family. I am thankful for my wonderful family, Doug, Sarah and Trina, who never let me lose sight of what is important in life...loved ones. ✦

TABLE OF CONTENTS

flowers for the BRIDE

PAGE 16

flowers for the WEDDING PARTY

PAGE 72

flowers for the CEREMONY AND RECEPTION

PAGE 92

INTRODUCTION

So you're getting married. Congratulations! The weeks and months that lie ahead will be filled with many exciting—and overwhelming—decisions. Nonetheless, this joyous time should be a memorable and pleasant experience for you and your loved ones.

There are so many things to consider when planning your wedding: budget, time of day, time of year, location, size and style to name a few. You want your wedding to reflect your taste and personality.

Within these pages, you will find an illustrated guide to unique, innovative, exciting and up-to-date wedding floral design. Whether you're working with a florist or handling the flower arrangements yourself, the easy, step-by-step instructions will teach you how to make a variety of colorful bridal bouquets, wedding party accessories, ceremony and reception decorations, and more!

If my twenty-plus years of experience in the floral design industry have taught me one thing, it is that no two weddings are alike. Therefore, I have chosen a variety of projects that represent every style. Whether your theme is classic, bold, extravagant, romantic, fun or elegant, you will surely find the perfect flower arrangements for your perfect day.

I hope you enjoy planning the wedding of your dreams as much as I have enjoyed writing this book. Best of luck to you now and in the future! ✦

wedding flower considerations

The key to successful wedding flowers is planning! Whether you design your own floral arrangements, have your florist create them or work in tandem with your florist, there are a few important issues you must consider.

1 BUDGET Don't be ashamed if you have a small budget. A good florist will make suggestions that work within your price range, no matter how big or small. Consider making some or all of the flowers yourself, or even growing them in your very own garden!

2 SIZE The size of your wedding party will greatly impact the amount of money you spend on flowers. Bouquets, corsages, boutonnieres and flower girl baskets add up, so you may want to limit the wedding party to include only your closest friends and family.

3 LOCATION Before choosing the location for your ceremony and reception, be sure to get all the information you need. Is the venue available on the date you have chosen? Do they have certain parameters when it comes to floral arrangements? Will you or the florist be able to arrive early to set up the arrangements?

4 COLOR SCHEME The color scheme of your wedding will be enhanced by the flowers you choose for the ceremony and reception. Look through books and magazines, and ask for advice from friends and family. Experiment with different types of flowers in a variety of colors until you have found the perfect combination.

5 PERSONAL STYLE Are you the serious type, or are you a comedian? Are you conservative or carefree? Your flowers should reflect your personality. Consider whether you prefer a simple bouquet of loose garden flowers or a sophisticated array of elegant blossoms.

6 MOOD Your flowers will not only reflect the color and style of the wedding, but they will also set the mood. Ask yourself what you want to convey on your wedding day. Attend other weddings and make mental notes about decorations that catch your eye, and why.

7 TIME OF DAY If you'd like your wedding to be more casual, consider holding the ceremony in the morning or afternoon. A simple bouquet of fresh wildflowers will enhance the casual yet classy wedding. If you are arranging your own flowers, consider scheduling your wedding later in the day to give yourself plenty of time for last-minute details.

8 WEATHER While nothing is more beautiful than an outdoor wedding, heat, wind and rain can put a damper on the day. If you're planning an outdoor summer wedding, choose flowers such as daisies, roses, lilies, carnations and mums. Avoid gardenias, tulips, stephanotis and irises, which are likely to wilt in high temperatures. For outdoor receptions, make sure your table arrangements are properly anchored. A light wind can easily blow them over.

9 SEASON To save money, choose flowers that are in season at the time of your wedding. Your florist will be able to help you with this and make suggestions based on your color, style and budget. Avoid ordering flowers during the holidays when they are in higher demand and will be more expensive. If out-of-season flowers are an absolute must, opt for silk arrangements instead.

10 FRAGRANCE The sweet aroma of your favorite flower can be beautiful, but it can also be overpowering. Use strong-smelling flowers such as gardenias, Stargazer lilies and Casa Blanca lilies sparingly, and ask your florist to recommend flowers with soft fragrances.

wedding flower plan

This guide will help you lay out your entire floral plan, including the budget and ordering quantities. Use it as a checklist to ensure that your wedding flower plan is as flawless as the beautiful blooms themselves.

bride

Color and style of dress	
Style of bouquet	
Types of flowers	
Price of bouquet	$
Price of tossing bouquet	$
Price of hairpiece/veil flowers	
TOTAL COST OF BRIDE'S FLOWERS	$

wedding party

Color and style of bridesmaids' dresses	
Style of bouquets	
Types of flowers	
Number of bridesmaids	
Price per bouquet	$
Total cost of bouquets	$

Color and style of flower girls' dresses	
Style of bouquets	
Types of flowers	
Number of flower girls	
Price per bouquet	$
Total cost of bouquets	$

Number of boutonnieres (include groom, fathers, best man, groomsmen, ushers, grandfathers, clergy and others)

Price per boutonniere	$
Total cost of boutonnieres	$

Number of corsages (include mothers, grandmothers, musicians, hostesses and honored guests)

Price per corsage	$
Total cost of corsages	$

TOTAL COST OF WEDDING PARTY'S FLOWERS	$

ceremony

Types of flowers	

Altar flowers	$
Aisle and pew decorations	$
Candelabra flowers	$
Other	$
TOTAL COST OF CEREMONY FLOWERS	$

reception

Types of flowers	

Number of guest tables	
Guest table flowers	$
Head table flowers	$
Total cost of table flowers	$

Cake table flowers	$
Cake flowers	$
Buffet table flowers	
Guest book table flowers	$
Gift table flowers	$
Other	$
TOTAL COST OF RECEPTION FLOWERS	$

TOTAL COST OF WEDDING FLOWERS	$

working with a florist

Although arranging your own flowers for your wedding is a great way to save money and ensure that you get exactly what you want, the task can be extremely overwhelming. Guidance from a professional florist will make the entire process run much more smoothly. Your florist should be able to answer your questions and make recommendations.

Choosing a professional florist isn't as easy as opening up the phone book and calling the first name you see. It is important to find a florist with whom you can communicate openly and discuss things like budget, expectations and responsibilities. Here are a few things to consider.

SHOP EARLY Begin your search for a professional florist about six months before your wedding. Make sure that the person you choose is willing to devote enough time to you during the planning stages and on that special day. Keep in mind that florists are often busier during holidays and in the summer, when weddings are more frequent.

SET A BUDGET Determine the amount you would like to spend on the bridal bouquet, wedding party flowers and ceremony and reception arrangements. Be leery of florists who try to steer you into a higher price range. A good florist will even suggest ways to cut costs, such as choosing in-season flowers.

BE PREPARED Before you meet with the florist, do your best to determine your wedding's theme and colors, time and date, ceremony and reception sites, size of the wedding party and number of guests. Bring pictures, color swatches, quotes from other florists and anything else that you think will convey your vision. A well-trained florist will listen to your comments and ask questions to help determine the overall plan.

PARTICIPATE Don't be afraid to express your ideas to your florist. A good florist will listen to your comments and work in conjunction with you.

DELEGATE RESPONSIBILITIES Create a list of the flowers you'd like to handle yourself, as well as the arrangements with which you would like the florist's help. For example, if you'd like to make the bridesmaids' bouquets and you'd like the florist to create boutonnieres to match, let the florist know. This will avoid the "who-does-what" questions that could reek havoc on your beautiful day.

ASK QUESTIONS Keep a running list of questions that you will want the florist to answer, such as: Is there a delivery charge and/or set-up fee? Will the bill be itemized? Are there any hidden costs?

DOCUMENT, DOCUMENT, DOCUMENT It is so important to keep accurate notes every time you meet with your florist. Write down everything from types of flowers to costs to ideas, and offer to make him or her a copy of your notes. A well-documented plan could mean the difference between an organized floral plan and a disaster!

floral basics: speaking the language of love

You'll want to educate yourself as much as possible before you meet with your florist and begin designing your flowers. The more you know, the more effectively you will be able to express your vision of the perfect wedding flowers. Here are a few important terms you'll need to know:

- **Cascade**—A traditional, full-flowing bouquet with long-stemmed flowers extended out to create a waterfall effect.
- **Nosegay**—A round bouquet (16" to 18" [41cm to 46cm] in diameter) with densely packed flowers.
- **Biedermeier**—A small nosegay composed of expanding rings of individual colors or flowers.

- **Hand-Tied**—A natural bouquet of flowers tied together with ribbons. Often the stems are left showing.
- **Pomander**—A flower-covered ball suspended from a loop of ribbon.
- **Tussie Mussie**—A hand-tied bouquet in which the flowers are tied together at the stems with ribbon trimmed to equal length.
- **Wired**—A bouquet in which each bloom is wired to stand upright and then bent into a desired shape.
- **Composite**—A bouquet assembled from flower petals that, when finished, appears to be one large blossom.
- **Round, Oval, Heart, Crescent**—These terms refer to the overall shape of the bouquet.

1. The Trailing Orchid Bouquet (page 62) is an example of a cascade.

2. The Glamellia Bouquet (page 42) is an example of a composite bouquet.

3. The flowergirl arrangement (page 86) is an example of a pomander.

4. The Pearl and Ribbon Bouquet (page 18) is an example of a Tussie Mussie.

basic tools and supplies

Before you roll up your sleeves and begin making the arrangements on the pages that follow, familiarize yourself with the basic tools and supplies you'll need.

✦ General Materials

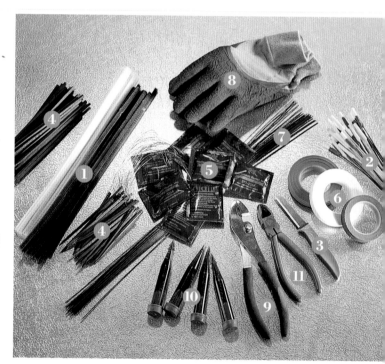

1. CHENILLE STEMS—Similar to pipe cleaners, these stems are used to secure bows and strengthen stems. They consist of bendable, twisted, heavy wire and a flocked material that allows water to flow through.

2. CORSAGE STEMS—These stems strengthen the ends of corsages so they can be held in place with pins.

3. CRAFT/PARING KNIFE—This is used for making precise cuts in materials such as vellum.

4. FLORAL PICKS—Wooden floral picks come in various sizes and are used to secure bows in bouquets and extend stem lengths. They are available with and without wire, as shown.

5. FLORAL PRESERVATIVES—These products contain vital plant nutrients to help your flowers stay fresher longer. They can be obtained from any florist.

6. FLORAL TAPE—This is used to wrap floral stems and bind flowers together. It is available in white, dark green and light green, and in various widths.

7. FLORAL WIRE—This wire comes in different weights, or gauges, and is used to strengthen stems and bind flowers together.

8. GARDEN GLOVES—Gloves are ideal for safely stripping thorns and unwanted leaves from stems.

9. PLIERS—These can be used for bending strong wire for a flower arrangement.

10. WATER TUBES—These tubes are filled with water and used to add fresh flowers to silk or dried bouquets as well as to potted plants. Water tubes are available in various lengths based on the size of the project and where they will be placed in the arrangement.

11. WIRE CUTTERS—These are used to cut thick stems and other heavy materials.

Foam and Holders

1. BOUQUET HOLDERS—Bouquet holders are available in many shapes and styles, including slanted-handle, straight-handle and Tussie Mussie holders. They can contain dry or wet foam.

2. FLORAL FOAM—There are two types of floral foam: dry and wet. Dry foam is for silk and dried flower projects and is firmer than wet foam. Wet foam, which we will use in this book, absorbs liquid to keep the stems moist and holds its shape when fresh flowers are arranged in it. It should be soaked very slowly. Be sure to float it on top of the water and let it absorb the water on its own. Oasis is a common brand of floral foam.

3. FOAM BALL—Foam balls are available in many diameters and in wet and dry forms. They are ideal for pomanders and topiaries.

4. FOAM RING—Foam rings come in many diameters and have a plastic backing for support. They can be used to make everything from door wreaths to candle rings and more.

5. ROUND IGLOO CAGES—These small round cages contain wet foam and are available in all different sizes. They are ideal for decorating cakes and centerpieces that do not require containers.

6. ROUND PLASTIC MESH CANVAS—Mesh canvases are ideal for making collars for floral arrangements.

Miscellaneous Supplies

1. CRAFT GLUE—Craft glue can be substituted for floral adhesives to secure floral materials and supplies.

2. DOUBLE-SIDED TAPE—This sticky adhesive fastens flowers and other supplies to themselves and to foam.

3. FLORAL ADHESIVE—Floral adhesive is a dependable glue for wet or dry surfaces. It does not require heating and dries clear. For best results, add to a surface and let sit until it is tacky before adhering anything to it. Oasis is a common floral adhesive brand.

4. HOT GLUE GUN—The hot glue from the glue gun is used to adhere flowers and other supplies to foam and to each other.

5. LEAF SHINE—Leaf shine is essential for cleaning foliage and giving it a waxy, crisp look. It also helps keep greenery from drying out too quickly. Common brands include Pokon and Crowning Glory.

6. SPRAY ADHESIVE—This is an aerosol spray that works best on dry surfaces. Common spray adhesive brands include Elmer's, Tack 2000, and FloraLock.

basic techniques

This section details some of the basic techniques of flower arranging that you will use throughout the book.

◆ wiring flowers

It is often necessary to wire flower stems to make them sturdier or to extend the length of the stems. Here is an easy way to prepare your stems.

1.   Insert a 6" (15cm) floral wire into the base of the flower head and pull it through. Leave equal lengths of wire on both sides of the flower base.

2.   Pull the ends of the wire down and in line with the stem to begin the wrapping process.

3.   Begin the wrapping process with floral tape, which does not have a right or wrong side. Floral tape becomes tacky and adheres to itself as it is stretched. Hold the flower with one hand and the tape with the other. Stretch and pull the tape downward, and twist the stem with the thumb and forefinger of one hand. As you twist, the tape should cover the stem and wires snugly, overlapping on its way down the stem.

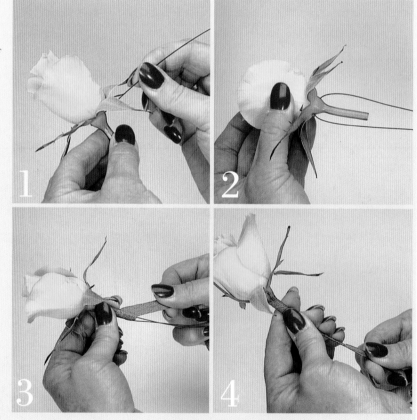

4.   Wrap the ends of the wire and press the tape snugly up and around to cover any exposed wire.

strengthening stems

Hollow-stemmed flowers such as gerbera daisies, daffodils and tulips will flop over quickly if the stems are not reinforced. Here's a florist's trick for keeping these flowers standing tall.

 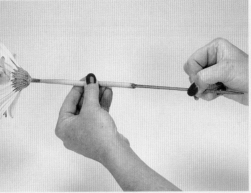

Insert the end of a chenille stem or floral pick into the base of the stem. Try to keep the flower's stem straight with one hand and slowly insert the chenille stem or floral pick with the other. You will not always be able to insert the chenille stem or floral pick all the way up the stem. Insert only until you feel resistance. Going up the stem even a third of the way will help strengthen the stem and keep it from prematurely wilting.

stripping thorns and leaves

Many types of flowers and foliage are very thorny, including roses, sprengeri and plumosa. Here's how to strip the stems of their thorns safely and quickly.

To remove thorns and clean stems safely, it is helpful to wear garden gloves. Hold the foliage or rose with one hand. With the other hand, grab the stem where you want to begin stripping the foliage and thorns and pull downward on the stem tightly.

cutting stems

For best results, cut flower stems at a slant while they are in water. For flowers such as roses and carnations, cut the stem above or below the noticeable nodules along the stems. This will allow water to easily reach the flower head. It will also help the flower to open fully.

preserving flowers

To keep your flowers looking good all day, hold the stems and dip the flower heads in a glue mixture of approximately one tablespoon of craft glue and one cup of water. Let dry for five minutes.

flowers for the BRIDE

1

More than any bridal accessory, your bridal bouquet will express the beauty and joy you are feeling on your wedding day. For years to come, the colors and fragrances will remind you of your special day. Your bouquet is the first thing your guests will see as you walk down the aisle, and it will be captured for a lifetime in your wedding photos.

It's easy to see how important choosing the right bouquet can be. Your flowers should complement your personality and work in harmony with your wedding style, not overpower it. Look at examples of bouquets from magazines, and attend bridal shows to gather ideas.

There are so many bouquet styles from which to choose—perhaps you'd like a snow-white trailing bouquet for a traditional ceremony, or a simple ribbon-wrapped bouquet for a more casual affair. Once you are set on a style, you must select your flowers. Your florist will be able to suggest flowers that are in season. Ultimately you want to weave all the aspects of your wedding—from dresses to bouquets to decorations— into a ceremony as exquisite as you are on your wedding day.

BOUQUET

This small bouquet of fragrant flowers, known as a Tussie Mussie, is the epitome of elegance. The pearls and ribbon used to accent the orchids, lisianthus blossoms and stephanotis are almost as beautiful as the flowers themselves.

fresh flowers

+ 4 PHALAENOPSIS ORCHIDS
+ 20 WHITE LISIANTHUS BLOSSOMS
+ 25-30 WHITE STEPHANOTIS (25 TO A BOX)

supplies

+ POSY POCKET TUSSIE MUSSIE
+ FLORAL FOAM BOUQUET HOLDER
+ 9" (23CM) ROUND PLASTIC MESH CANVAS
+ 4 YARDS (3.6M) OF 2¼" (6CM) WIDE WHITE WIRED RIBBON
+ 14' (4.3M) OF SHEER WHITE PEARL-EDGED RIBBON
+ 2 STRANDS OF PEARLS MEASURING AT LEAST 12" (30CM) IN LENGTH
+ 18 STRANDS OF PEARLS MEASURING 8" (20CM) IN LENGTH
+ PEARL CORSAGE PINS
+ WHITE STEPHANOTIS STEMS
+ WIRED WOODEN FLORAL PICKS
+ WHITE FLORAL TAPE
+ COTTON FLORAL STEMS
+ FLORAL ADHESIVE
+ HOT GLUE GUN
+ CRAFT KNIFE

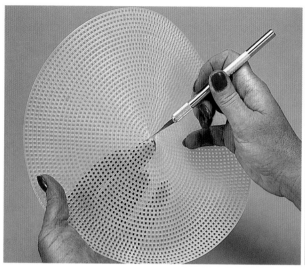

cut hole in canvas center

Cut an X into the center of a 9" (23cm) round 7-mesh canvas with a craft knife.

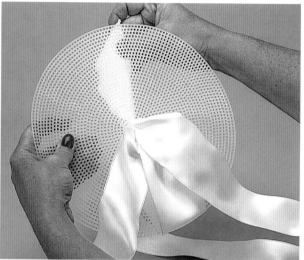

cover canvas with ribbon

Loop the white wired ribbon through the center of the hole, around the outside of the canvas and back through to cover the mesh.

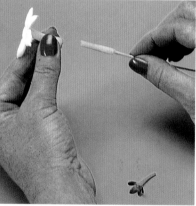

secure ribbon ends

Glue down the ribbon ends with floral adhesive to secure them to the mesh as shown. Submerge the floral holder into water for ten minutes. Push the handle of the floral bouquet holder through the center of the ribbon collar. Using a hot glue gun, secure the base of the holder into the collar.

prepare stephanotis blossoms

Remove the small green stems and centers from the stephanotis blossoms. Immerse the cotton floral stems in water for a few seconds and insert them into the bottom center of each blossom.

insert pearl

Trim a pearl corsage pin to ½" (13mm) and insert it into the top center of each blossom. If needed, add a dab of glue to secure.

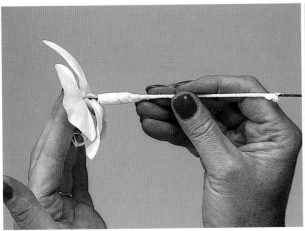

prepare phalaenopsis orchids

Insert the cotton stems into the base of each phalaenopsis stem and flower to secure. These orchids are very fragile, so handle with care.

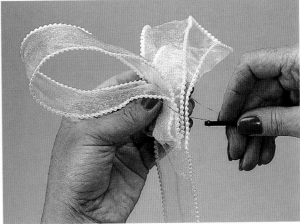

make ribbon picks

Using the pearl-edged ribbon, form two loops 5" to 6" (13cm to 15cm) long. Cut the end of the second loop about 1" (3cm) longer than the base of the loop. Twist the wire of a 3" (8cm) wooden pick around the ends of the loops as shown, and secure tightly to the pick. Make six more.

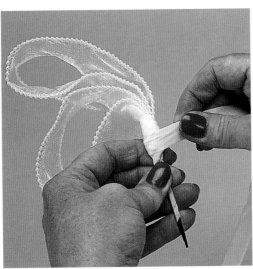

wrap wooden picks

Wrap the wire tightly to the picks with white floral tape. Pull and stretch.

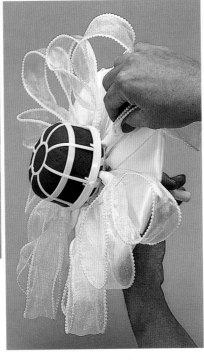

insert picks

Insert the seven picks into the floral foam, spacing them evenly around the edge of the bouquet.

add phalaenopsis orchids

Insert the orchid stems into the center of the bouquet holder. Arrange two close together and two farther apart. Secure with floral adhesive.

add lisianthus blossoms

Randomly insert 20 open lisianthus blossoms with 2" to 4" (5cm to 10cm) stems throughout the bouquet.

add stephanotis

Wrap three stems of stephanotis into a cluster with white floral tape. Repeat with the remaining stephanotis stems. Insert the clusters randomly throughout the bouquet and at various depths. Allow some of the stems to stick out from the other flowers for a looser appearance.

prepare short pearl strands

Cluster three to six short pearl strands, twist them together and attach them to a wired wooden pick.

secure strands

Wrap the pearl strands and wooden pick with white floral tape.

insert short pearl strands

Randomly insert the short pearl clusters into the bouquet.

insert long pearl strands

Wire the two long strands of pearls onto the wooden picks and wrap with white floral tape. Insert the strands, staggered, into only one side of the bouquet at the base. The longest strand should be 14" (36cm) long.

insert and secure handle

When the ribbon is completely dry, spray the base of the bouquet and the handle with spray adhesive. Insert the handle into the center of the Tussie Mussie.

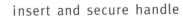

TO ENSURE freshness, make this bouquet no more than one day in advance. Stephanotis and phalaenopsis orchids are fragile flowers that can bruise easily. They need special care in handling and refrigeration. Should a few of the stephanotis blossoms look brown on your wedding day, simply remove them from the bouquet. They won't be missed since the flowers are so numerous and full. ✦

gardenia tassel

BOUQUET

This bouquet is a beautiful array of gardenias, plum miniature calla lilies and rhinestone ribbon roses. For a special touch, decorative ribbon loops and tassels were also added.

fresh flowers

- 7 GARDENIAS WITH SILK LEAVES
- 7 PLUM MINIATURE CALLA LILIES

supplies

- SLANTED-HANDLE BOUQUET HOLDER
- 12 YARDS (11M) OF 1½" (4CM) WIDE SPRING MOSS DOUBLE-FACED SATIN RIBBON
- 30 WHITE SATIN RIBBON ROSES WITH RHINESTONE CENTERS
- 2 WHITE DECORATIVE CORDS WITH TASSELS ON EACH END
- FLORAL WIRE
- WIRED WOODEN FLORAL PICKS
- WHITE AND GREEN FLORAL TAPE
- CRAFT GLUE
- FLORAL ADHESIVE
- WIRE CUTTERS

make bow

Make a center loop of a bow using 7' (2m) of ribbon. Twist the ribbon to form a medium hoop. Pinch the ribbon together in the center with your fingers. Make eight loops in all, twisting the ribbon in the center before each loop.

secure bow

Secure the bow by wrapping the wire attached to the floral pick around the middle of the bow. Twist tightly.

tape bow

Secure the bow to the pick by wrapping green floral tape around the wire at the base of the bow and partly down the floral pick. Twist and pull the tape tightly as you wrap. Repeat the process to make four additional bows, finishing the ribbon ends with angled cuts.

add bows

Submerge the bouquet holder in water for ten minutes. Insert one bow into the center of the bouquet holder. Insert the remaining four bows around the perimeter. For a fuller, finished bouquet, fluff the ribbon loops with your hands.

wire gardenias

Insert two thin floral wires in opposite directions through the base of each gardenia. Wrap the wires around the stem once, then bend them down to extend the stem.

protect gardenias

Protect the gardenias with a solution of glue and water. Mix six parts water to one part glue in a bowl. Dip the gardenias into the solution and set aside to dry.

wrap gardenias

Wrap the wire from the base of the gardenia stem with white floral tape. Pull and stretch the tape tightly as it is wrapped. Trim the wire stem to 1½" (4cm) in length using wire cutters.

attach pick

Attach a floral pick to the gardenia stem by wrapping the wire around the stem. Secure with white floral tape.

add gardenias

Insert one gardenia stem into the center of the bouquet.
Next, insert three gardenias around the center gardenia in
the formation of a triangle. Insert and stagger the last three
gardenias among the ones in the triangle to create a round
bouquet look.

add calla lilies

Trim the miniature calla lily stems to 3" (8cm) in length.
Insert randomly throughout the bouquet.

prepare tassels

Gather the cords of the
tassels in one hand and
arrange at desired lengths.

prepare ribbon roses

Make ten clusters of three ribbon roses and
secure them onto a wired floral pick. To do this,
wrap the wire around the ribbon rose stems and
secure with white floral tape. Insert the ribbon
rose clusters randomly throughout the bouquet.

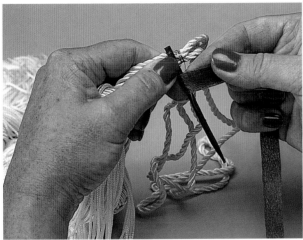

secure tassels

Secure the tassels at the desired lengths by wrapping the wire from a floral pick around the cords. Twist the wire tightly to hold.

add tassels

Insert the floral pick holding the tassels into the lowest part of the holder. Use floral adhesive to secure them.

✦
MAKE THIS BOUQUET no more than a day in advance. Gardenias bruise and brown very easily. When you purchase the gardenias, be sure to keep them in the refrigerator, packaged in a sealed container. Touch up brown edges by carefully applying off-white paint with a soft brush. ✦

BOUQUET

In this bouquet, fresh green ivy works its way around the base of the holder, forming a collar on which the field flowers rest. A variety of blooms in similar shades of purple create an English feel for this bouquet.

fresh flowers

- 1 GREEN IVY PLANT WITH TRAILERS
- 1 PURPLE VIOLET PLANT
- 10 STEMS OF PURPLE VERONICA
- 7 PURPLE ANEMONES
- 5 STEMS OF PURPLE LISIANTHUS
- 3 STEMS OF PURPLE WAXFLOWER

supplies

- STRAIGHT-HANDLED BOUQUET HOLDER
- 8" (21CM) ROUND PLASTIC MESH CANVAS
- 3" (8CM) WIRED WOODEN FLORAL PICKS
- FLORAL FOAM
- THIN FLORAL WIRE OR CHENILLE STEM
- DOUBLE-SIDED TAPE
- SPRAY ADHESIVE
- FLORAL ADHESIVE OR HOT GLUE GUN
- CRAFT KNIFE

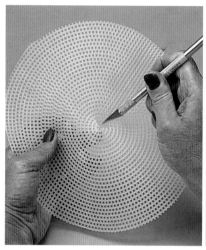

cut mesh canvas

Using a craft knife, cut a 1" (3cm) slit in the form of an X through the center of the mesh canvas.

cover bottom

Use spray adhesive to secure the ivy leaves to the back of the canvas, leaving a small space in the center at the X.

wire violet blossoms

Cut four or five clusters of violet blossoms, stems included. Wire them onto the 3" (8cm) wooden floral picks. Violet stems are very fragile, so handle with care.

secure holder

Insert the holder into the center of the mesh canvas at the X. Secure it with double-sided tape.

insert violet clusters

Submerge the holder in water for ten minutes and allow to dry. Insert the violets into the center of the foam.

cover handle

Cover the bouquet handle and the opening in the canvas with ivy leaves and secure with spray adhesive.

add flowers

Insert ten sprigs of purple veronica, seven sprigs of anemones and five sprigs of lisianthus, each with 2" (5cm) stems, randomly throughout the bouquet. To strengthen the stems, insert a thin floral wire or chenille stem. Next, add several sprigs of purple waxflower with 1" (3cm) stems amid the other flowers. For a more tailored look, trim off the rugged ends of the waxflower.

THE IVY COLLAR CLUTCH BOUQUET can be made a couple of days in advance. Be sure to use the spray adhesive sparingly, as this bouquet doesn't require a lot of glue to secure. Place the bouquet in a cool place or in the refrigerator, and cover with a plastic bag. Don't forget that in the winter months, flowers can be stored in the garage at 30° F (1° C). ✦

victorian holiday

BOUQUET

This brilliant and elegant bouquet is simple to make and rich in presentation. It's perfect for a Christmas or Valentine's Day wedding. The beautiful arrangement includes red miniature gerbera daisies, bright red roses, seeded eucalyptus and red hypericum berries.

fresh flowers

- 9 RED MINIATURE GERBERA DAISIES
- 8 BRIGHT RED ROSES
- 5 RED ANEMONES
- 2 STEMS OF SEEDED EUCALYPTUS
- 2-3 STEMS OF MING FERN

silk flowers

- 7 RED HYPERICUM BERRY CLUSTERS

supplies

- SILVER TUSSIE MUSSIE BOUQUET HOLDER
- LEAF SHINE

1. add seeded eucalyptus

Soak the bouquet holder in water for ten minutes. Cut several sprigs of seeded eucalyptus, each with 1" (3cm) stems. Trim half of the foliage off the stems, leaving the berries. (In my opinion, minimal leaves look better in this bouquet.) Insert the sprigs of seeded eucalyptus in the holder to cover completely. Spray with leaf shine to eliminate the gray look of the eucalyptus.

add ming fern

Add sprigs of ming fern, each with 1" (3cm) stems, randomly throughout the bouquet.

add roses

Add eight red roses, each with 3" (8cm) stems, randomly throughout the bouquet. Start with one in the center.

add gerbera daisies

Add nine gerbera daisies, each with 3" (8cm) stems, randomly throughout the bouquet. Be sure to balance your placement with the roses.

add anemones

Add five anemones, each with 3" (8cm) stems, randomly throughout the bouquet.

add red berries

Add seven red berry clusters, each with 3" (8cm) stems, throughout the bouquet. To add depth and visual appeal, you may wish to arrange additional roses around the outside of the bouquet.

◆ YOU CAN MAKE this bouquet a couple of days before the wedding if you keep it standing upright in a vase and store it in a cool place. To keep your flowers fresher longer, dilute a packet of nutrient-rich floral preservatives in water and mist over the flowers with a spray bottle. Crystal Clear is a popular brand preservative that can be found in most floral shops. ◆

BOUQUET

This luscious bouquet, filled with green flowers,

incorporates orchids, hydrangea, hypericum berries

and exotic foliage for a contemporary appearance.

Trailing greenery gives the look of a cascading waterfall.

fresh flowers

+ 6 GREEN CYMBIDIUM ORCHID BLOSSOMS
+ 2-3 GREEN HYDRANGEAS
+ 4 STEMS OF GREEN CAMELLIA FOLIAGE
+ 8 STEMS OF LILY GRASS
+ 5 STEMS OF MING FERN
+ 8 STEMS OF GREEN HYPERICUM BERRIES

supplies

+ SLANTED-HANDLE BOUQUET HOLDER
+ 6 GREEN CORSAGE STEMS
+ LEAF SHINE
+ FLORAL ADHESIVE

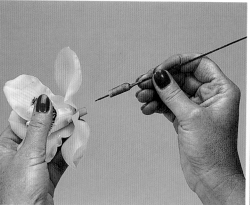

add ming fern

Submerge the bouquet holder in water for ten minutes. Cut five sprigs of ming fern measuring 6" to 10" (15cm to 25cm) in length. For easy insertion into the foam, remove any foliage or leaves from the bottom of the sprig, leaving a 1" (3cm) stem. Add the longest sprigs at the bottom of the bouquet as trailers. Spray with leaf shine to preserve the foliage.

prepare orchids

Trim the cymbidium orchid stems to ½" (13mm) in length. Submerge the cotton portion of the corsage stems in water and insert them into the base of the orchid stems. The cotton will absorb the water and keep the bouquet hydrated.

insert orchids

Insert the six orchids into the bouquet holder at different angles, making an oval shape. Orchids are extremely fragile, so handle with care.

add hydrangea

Cut stems of green hydrangea into 2" to 4" (5cm to 10cm) long sprigs. Insert them randomly throughout the bouquet.

secure orchids

Secure the orchids with floral adhesive. Apply the glue where the stem and the foam meet.

add camellia foliage

Cut stems of camellia foliage into sprigs measuring 6" to 15" (15cm to 38cm) in length. Wipe any dirt from the leaves and spray with leaf shine. Insert the longer sprigs into the top and bottom of the bouquet. Insert the remaining sprigs randomly throughout the bouquet.

insert hypericum berries

Trim eight stems of green hypericum berries, each with 2" (5cm) stems, and insert randomly throughout the bouquet. Next, insert eight stems of lily grass into the top and bottom of the bouquet. Spray both with leaf shine to add a glossy finish.

FEEL FREE TO MAKE

to make this bouquet a few days in advance. Keep extra hydrangea stems on hand just in case they wilt prematurely. To assist with the hydration of the hydrangeas before they are inserted into the bouquet, cut the stems at a slant numerous times and place back in water. Be sure to store this bouquet in a cool place. ✦

glamellia

BOUQUET

This is a composite bouquet in which individual gladiola petals are fastened together to create a single giant glamellia blossom. By adding just a bit of greenery and a decorative ribbon, you will further enhance this bouquet's exceptionally stunning simplicity.

fresh flowers

- 3-5 WHITE GLADIOLAS WITH OPEN BLOSSOMS
- 1 BUNCH OF GALAX LEAVES
- 4-5 STEMS OF MAIDENHAIR FERN

supplies

- 6" (16CM) ROUND PLASTIC MESH CANVAS
- 6 YARDS (5M) OF 2¼" (6CM) WIDE SHEER WHITE RIBBON
- 18" (46CM) THIN FLORAL WIRE
- WHITE CHENILLE STEMS
- LEAF SHINE
- WHITE FLORAL TAPE
- CLEAR LIQUID SHIELD SPRAY
- SPRAY ADHESIVE
- CRAFT KNIFE

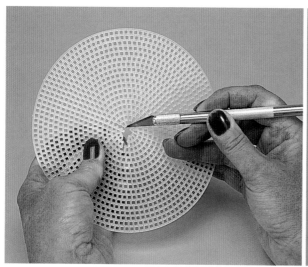

cut center of canvas

Using a craft knife, cut a 1" (3cm) X into the center of the plastic mesh canvas.

outline topside of canvas

Using spray adhesive, individually spray each galax leaf and secure around the top perimeter of the mesh canvas. Spray the foliage with leaf shine to add a glossy look.

cover underside of canvas

Using spray adhesive, cover the underside of the mesh canvas. Allow an opening at the X.

trim gladiola blossoms

Gently pull the open blossoms from the gladiola stems with your hands.

make bouquet center

Insert wire through the base of three full gladiola blossoms. Group the blossoms together and gather wires.

bind blossoms together

Using two to three layers of white floral tape, cover the wired stems.

add chenille stems

Bend two chenille stems in the center and push the ends through the mesh canvas on either side of the X.

insert gladiola

Insert the gladiola blossom cluster through the X. Floral tape the wired and chenille stems together and repeat.

add gladiola petals

Delicately separate individual petals from the remaining gladiola blossoms, being careful not to crease them. Using spray adhesive, glue each individual petal to the base of the bouquet. Start adding petals directly underneath the center cluster in a circular pattern, layering tightly.

finish outside layers

Continue in a circular pattern, layering the petals until only the outside edges of the galax leaves are showing. You can also outline the perimeter with other foliage such as rich green camellia leaves.

create bow

Use 3 yards (3m) of 2¼" (6cm) sheer white ribbon to create a bow. Start with 4" (10cm) loops, gradually making them larger. Create eight loops, holding the bow with one hand and forming the loops with the other. Cut 3 additional yards (3m) of ribbon to create longer loops for the look of streamers. Attach the bow and streamers with a chenille stem.

attach bow to bouquet

Using white floral tape, attach the bow to the stem of the bouquet. Pull and stretch the floral tape tightly when combining the chenille stem from the bow to the artificial stem you made for the bouquet.

13. add maidenhair fern

Gather four to five stems of maidenhair fern at staggered lengths to form a cluster. Secure with a chenille stem twisted around the cluster. Wrap the chenille stem tightly with floral tape as shown.

14. attach fern to bouquet

Attach the chenille stem from the cluster of maidenhair fern just below the bow with white floral tape. Wrap tightly several times and pull the tape over the end to hide any exposed wire. The stem of the bouquet becomes the handle. Cover with satin ribbon if desired.

THIS BOUQUET can be made a couple of days in advance. Spray the gladiola petals with a clear liquid shield to seal in moisture and protect them from wilting prematurely. Store in a cool place and do not touch the flower petals so as not to bruise them. ✦

exotic calla lily

BOUQUET

The calla lily represents magnificent beauty, sophistication and elegance.

With just a few fresh flowers and basic supplies, you can create this

breathtaking bouquet to add dramatic flair to your wedding day.

fresh flowers

+ 10 YELLOW MINIATURE CALLA LILIES
+ 5 GINGER LEAVES

supplies

+ SPRAY ADHESIVE
+ ½" (13MM) GREEN WATERPROOF TAPE
+ LEAF SHINE
+ PARING KNIFE
+ CRAFT SCISSORS

gather calla lilies

Gather the miniature calla lilies in your hand at staggered heights. Arrange the lilies with longer stems in the back and the lilies with shorter stems in the front. For a smaller and less expensive bouquet, as few as three miniature calla lilies can be used.

prepare ginger leaves

Snip off the base of the ginger leaves and spray the leaves with leaf shine.

trim ginger leaves

If necessary, trim the apex of the back of the leaves so they are smoother and more pliable. Use a paring knife to lightly shave off the excess.

surround calla lilies

Surround the calla lilies with one ginger leaf, positioned vertically in the back of the blossoms. Make sure the shiny side is facing the flowers. Place another leaf behind the first leaf with the shiny side exposed and the dull side touching the original leaf. Wrap the base of the leaves around the stems of the calla lilies and secure with waterproof tape. Allow the tape to overlap, as it does not adhere well to leaf shine products.

wrap stem base

Add another ginger leaf to wrap around the base of the stems. Wrap the dull side of the leaf facing out. Secure with waterproof tape in two places.

add angled ginger leaves

Position a ginger leaf so that it is angled to the left with the matte side facing out. Wrap the end of the leaf around the stems and secure it with spray adhesive.

add final leaf

Wrap the bottom of the remaining ginger leaf around the back of the stems to the left and around the base of the stems to the right. Secure with spray adhesive. To finish the bouquet, trim the stems evenly at the bottom.

◆

MAKE THIS BOUQUET no more than one day before the wedding to ensure freshness. Store the bouquet upright in a cool place with a touch of water in the vase for the stems. Do not fill the vase with water, as the leaves may not stay secure when wet that long. This bouquet is very hardy and is not as fragile as others. ◆

rosy biedermeier

BOUQUET

The Biedermeier bouquet style, which originated in Austria, gained popularity during the late seventeenth and early eighteenth centuries. This pastel bouquet is soft and feminine in color, yet compact and sturdy in construction. The stephanotis, spray roses, mums, baby's breath, hypericum berries, Queen Anne's lace and galax leaves are layered from inside out to form a compact, sphere-like appearance.

fresh flowers

+ 12 STEPHANOTIS BLOSSOMS
+ 5-6 STEMS OF PEACH SPRAY ROSES
+ 15 WHITE ROSES
+ 4-5 STEMS OF GREEN BUTTON MUMS
+ 6-8 STEMS OF GREEN HYPERICUM BERRIES
+ 5-6 STEMS OF QUEEN ANNE'S LACE
+ 1-2 STEMS OF BABY'S BREATH
+ 8-10 GALAX LEAVES

supplies

+ SLANTED-HANDLE BOUQUET HOLDER
+ GREEN STEPHANOTIS STEMS
+ PEARL CORSAGE PINS
+ LEAF SHINE
+ FLORAL ADHESIVE
+ SPRAY ADHESIVE

insert stephanotis

Submerge the holder in water for ten minutes. Insert a stephanotis stem into each blossom. Trim the corsage pins to 1" (3cm) and insert into the blossom centers. Trim the stephanotis stems to 2½" (6cm) and insert into the holder.

add baby's breath

Cut off sprigs of baby's breath with 1" to 2" (3cm to 5cm) stems. Insert the sprigs tightly around the stephanotis.

add spray roses

Cut 16 to 18 spray roses (each stem contains 3 to 4 roses), each with 2½" (6cm) stems. Insert them around the perimeter of the baby's breath.

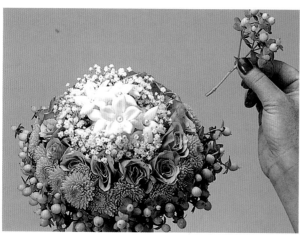

add hypericum berries

Insert the button mums around the spray roses. Cut sprigs of hypericum berries, each with 2" to 3" (5cm to 8cm) stems. Remove some of the leaves for easier insertion. Insert the berry stems around the perimeter of the button mums. Gradually insert each flower row lower than the last. This will keep your bouquet from appearing flat.

add white roses

Cut the stems of each rose to measure 3" (8cm) in length. Insert them around the perimeter of the hypericum berries. This row of roses will be the widest part of the bouquet. Use floral adhesive to secure the stems.

add galax leaves

Spray the galax leaves with leaf shine. Cut the stems off of the leaves and spray the backs of the leaves and bouquet holder with spray adhesive. Secure the leaves to the holder to finish the bouquet. The handle of the holder can also be covered with leaves.

add queen anne's lace

Cut several sprigs of Queen Anne's lace, each with 3" (8cm) stems. Insert deeply around the underneath perimeter of the roses. Finish the back of the bouquet holder with the Queen Anne's lace. Use floral adhesive to secure the stems.

ARRANGE THIS BOUQUET one day before the wedding and store it in the refrigerator. Secure the stems well so that they don't slip out of the foam. If you wish to use other flowers as substitutes, consider their size. For example, tulips can open up flat in warm temperatures and may, therefore, be too large. ◆

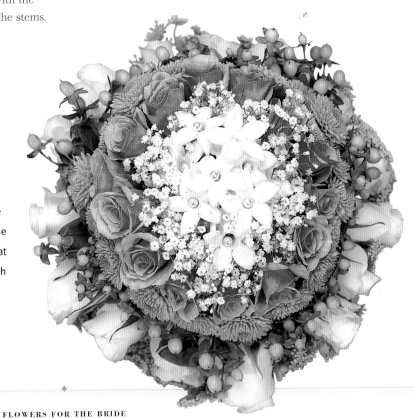

autumn daisy

BOUQUET

Autumn is a time when some of nature's most brilliant colors

present themselves. The fiery reds, vibrant oranges, rich purples

and radiant golds in this bouquet represent the best that nature

has to offer in florals during this beautiful season.

fresh flowers

+ 1 BUNCH OF GREEN MYRTLE
+ 5 RED MINIATURE GERBERA DAISIES
+ 2 ORANGE MINIATURE GERBERA DAISIES
+ 3 BRIGHT YELLOW ROSES
+ 3 STEMS OF BURNT ORANGE WAXFLOWER
+ 3 STEMS OF PURPLE STATICE

supplies

+ COPPER BEAD WIRE
+ FLORAL ADHESIVE OR HOT GLUE GUN
+ HEAVY-DUTY WIRE CUTTERS

remove leaves

Remove the leaves from the bottom third of the myrtle stems. Gather the stems to form a full bouquet.

trim ends

Using heavy-duty wire cutters, cut the stems evenly to measure 5" (13cm) in length.

secure stems

Secure the stems tightly by wrapping them with the copper bead wire and twisting to anchor the wire in place.

wrap stems

Continue to wrap the stems tightly with the copper wire until 3" (8cm) of the stems are covered.

trim myrtle

Trim the top of the myrtle until it is flat, similar to a hedge.

glue in waxflower

Glue and randomly insert the waxflower stems into the foliage at the top and sides of the bouquet.

trim waxflower

Trim the waxflower so that the bouquet still has a flat, hedge-like appearance.

add yellow roses

Cut three yellow roses with 4" (10cm) stems, apply glue to the stems and insert them into the top of the bouquet in a triangular pattern.

add gerbera daisies

Cut two orange and five red miniature gerbera daisies with 4" (10cm) stems, apply glue to the stems and insert them on opposite sides of the bouquet.

add purple statice

Cut sprigs of statice, measuring 3" (8cm) in length, from two to three stems. Apply glue to the stems and randomly insert them throughout the bouquet.

add more waxflower

Cut sprigs measuring 3" (8cm) in length from one stem of waxflower. Apply glue to the stems and insert them along the sides of the bouquet.

◆ ALTHOUGH IT has no water source, you can still make this hardy bouquet up to one day before your wedding. When securing the flowers into the greens of the bouquet, the glue will help to seal moisture into the stems of the flowers. It can also be misted if desired. ◆

garden-inspired

BOUQUET

This delightful bouquet, inspired by the garden, is wonderful for weddings in the budding spring or sunny summer. The hand-gathered design has a casual, carefree feel, excellent for almost any style of event.

fresh flowers

- 6 STEMS OF PINK LISIANTHUS
- 5 PINK TULIPS
- 5 STEMS OF PINK WAXFLOWER
- 3 PLUM HYDRANGEAS
- 5 STEMS OF QUEEN'ANNE'S LACE

supplies

- 24" (61CM) OF 1½" (4CM) WIDE WIRED LAVENDER RIBBON
- 4 PEARL CORSAGE PINS
- ½" (13MM) WIDE GREEN WATERPROOF TAPE

arrange waxflower and hydrangeas

Remove the lower foliage from the hydrangea stems. Arrange five stems of pink waxflower in a loose and airy style. Insert one stem of hydrangea into the center of the bouquet and insert the remaining two off center and lower in the bouquet cluster.

add lisianthus

Add six stems of lisianthus randomly around the outside of the bouquet.

add queen anne's lace

Hold the bouquet loosely in your hand. Insert five stems of Queen Anne's lace randomly throughout the bouquet.

add tulips

Insert five tulips randomly throughout the bouquet. For a more natural look, allow them to fall outward. The tulips should be placed lower than actually wanted. This is because they tend to grow a few inches overnight when placed in water.

trim stems

Trim all of the stems to measure about 8" (20cm) in length.

secure bouquet

Using a 16" (41cm) strip of waterproof tape, secure the bouquet by wrapping downward about 1" (3cm) around the stems. Wrap the base of the flowers.

add ribbon accent

Wrap the taped area of the stems with ribbon several times. Fold the end of the ribbon under and secure it with four pearl corsage pins. Insert the corsage pins downward through the ribbon end and into the center of the stem cluster.

◆

THIS BOUQUET can be arranged days before the wedding when stored upright and in a cool place. Because tulips tend to grow quickly, you may want to trim the stems shorter to allow for the growth if preparing a few days in advance. Do not place the bouquet in bright light. ◆

RIBBON-WRAPPING *techniques*

The radiant bride deserves a bouquet equally as beautiful. Wrap your favorite ribbon around the stems of fresh flowers for a simple, yet elegant, look. Try one of these ribbon-wrapping techniques, or be creative and design your own fancy dressing for your bouquet.

supplies

+ RIBBON OF YOUR CHOICE
+ GREEN WATERPROOF FLORAL TAPE
+ CORSAGE PINS

Simple Bow Technique

1. secure stems

Wrap the stems at the top, middle and 1" (3cm) above the end of the stems with floral tape. Space evenly.

2. create bows

Cut three strands of ribbon to measure 18" (46cm) in length. Wrap each strand around the stems where they are taped. Tie each ribbon into a shoestring-type bow and double knot. Trim the ribbon ends to the desired length.

Twisted Ribbon Technique

1 wrap stems

Wrap the stems together with floral tape. Trim a piece of ribbon to at least twice the length of the stems. Begin by wrapping the ribbon around the stems at the base. Twist by criss-crossing the ribbon ends.

2 continue twisting ribbon

Continue wrapping and twisting the ends all the way up the stems. Secure at the top with a double knot and trim the ends.

Full Stem-Wrapping Technique

1 start wrap

Wrap the stems together with waterproof floral tape. Cut a piece of ribbon measuring at least twice the length of the stems. Begin by wrapping the ribbon around the stems at the base and continue upward.

2 secure wrapped ribbon

When the stems have been completely wrapped, trim off any excess ribbon. Fold the ribbon end under and insert three corsage pins through the end and into the middle of the stems laterally to secure.

flowers for the WEDDING PARTY

Just as a fine wine complements a delicious meal, the wedding party's flowers should enhance the bridal bouquet. Once you have chosen your bouquet, you are ready to select the arrangements for the friends and loved ones in your wedding party.

Choosing a signature flower as the focal point of your bouquet will establish an overall theme for the wedding party's flowers. A simple bridal bouquet of five long-stemmed white roses, for instance, would go wonderfully with bridesmaids' bouquets of three long-stemmed dark red roses. Likewise, boutonnieres could follow suit with a white rosebud for the groom and dark red rosebuds for the groomsmen. The flowers and colors should complement each other, but your bouquet should stand out among those of your friends and family.

No one can resist an adorable flower girl or ringbearer. But along with sweet little smiles come little hands, legs and feet. Be sure to select accessories that are easy to carry down the aisle. When choosing an accessory for the flower girl, many brides opt for a miniature version of their own bouquet. In this case, be sure that it is light enough to hold throughout the entire ceremony.

Finally, choose arrangements that will look good in pictures. White flowers tend to look green when photographed in bright light. Also, be sure to choose flowers that won't blend in with your bridesmaids' dresses. Although your special day will fly by, your pictures are memories that you will treasure forever.

hydrangea and rose

CORSAGE and BOUTONNIERE

The perfect corsage or boutonniere will make each person in your wedding party feel like an integral part of your special day. Each of these simple and elegant pieces includes a hydrangea blossom, a spray rose and greenery to set off the delicate flowers.

fresh flowers

+ 2 BLUE HYDRANGEA BLOSSOMS
+ 2 YELLOW SPRAY ROSES
+ 2 STEMS OF SEEDED EUCALYPTUS
+ 2 STEMS OF RUSCUS GREENERY
+ 1 BUNCH OF LILY GRASS

supplies

+ 15" (38CM) OF 5/8" (16MM) WIDE OFF-WHITE SATIN RIBBON
+ 6" (15CM) OF 3/8" (10MM) WIDE OFF-WHITE SATIN RIBBON
+ CORSAGE PIN
+ BOUTONNIERE PIN
+ FLORAL WIRE
+ GREEN FLORAL TAPE
+ WIRE CUTTERS

corsage

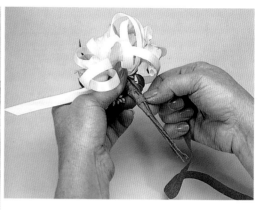

prepare flower clusters

Trim the stem of a yellow spray rose and a hydrangea blossom to measure 1" (3cm) each. Trim small sprigs of ruscus and seeded eucalyptus from each stem. Insert a thin floral wire through the center of this cluster and bend in half. Secure with floral tape. Pull and wrap the tape tightly around the stems. Make two more clusters.

prepare bow

Cut a piece of ⅝" (16mm) ribbon to measure approximately 15" (38cm) in length. Beginning about 4" (10cm) from the end of the ribbon strand, make five to six loops measuring 2" (5cm) in length. Secure by inserting a floral wire through the center of the bow and twisting tightly around the ribbon. Wrap the wire with green floral tape.

add lily grass

Cut three sprigs of lily grass. Place one sprig in the back of the cluster and loop two sprigs into the cluster. Secure with floral tape. Using wire cutters, trim the stems of the corsage to approximately 2" to 3" (5cm to 8cm). Insert a corsage pin into the stem so that it is handy to pin on.

add flower clusters

Place the flower clusters around the bow and secure with floral tape.

boutonniere

prepare
hydrangea blossom

Insert a floral wire into the center of the hydrangea blossom and bend it in half to secure the blossom to the wire. Wrap the entire wire and the small hydrangea stem with floral tape.

prepare
eucalyptus and ruscus

Place a sprig of ruscus behind a sprig of seeded eucalyptus. Insert a floral wire through the cluster and bend in half. Fasten the sprigs together by wrapping with the floral tape.

add lily grass

Trim two sprigs of lily grass to measure 4" (10cm) in length. Place the lily grass tip behind the ruscus. Form a loop with the other sprig and place it on one side of the greenery cluster. Secure with floral tape.

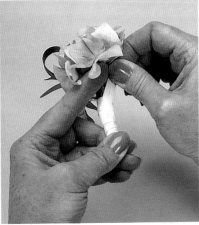

add rose and hydrangea

Trim the stem of the yellow spray roses to measure 1" (3cm) in length. Place the rose and hydrangea blossoms in the center of the greenery cluster and secure with floral tape. Trim the stem of the boutonniere to approximately 2" (5cm) in length.

tie off ribbon end

Wrap 6" (15cm) of ⅜" (10mm) ribbon up to the stem to completely cover it. Pull the last wrap tightly with the end of the ribbon slipped under the last loop.

secure ribbon

Fasten the ribbon in place by inserting a boutonniere pin through the ribbon end into the center of the floral wrapped stem.

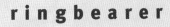

ringbearer
PILLOW

This simple yet stunning pillow features hydrangeas,

gerbera daisies and freesia in a mix of bright and sunny colors.

Won't it look lovely holding your sparkling rings on your wedding day?

fresh flowers

+ 1 PURPLE HYDRANGEA BLOSSOM
+ 1 YELLOW GERBERA DAISY
+ 1 STEM OF YELLOW FREESIA
+ 1 STEM OF WHITE FREESIA

supplies

+ 15" X 6" (38CM X 15CM)
  SACHET PILLOW
+ 3 YARDS (3M) OF 1½" (4CM) WIDE
  YELLOW SHEER RIBBON
+ 9 YARDS (8M) OF 1½" (4CM) WIDE
  MOSS GREEN SATIN RIBBON
+ HOT GLUE GUN
+ STAPLER

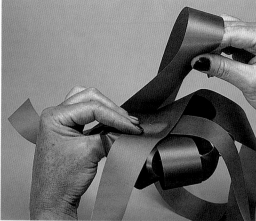

make bow chain

Using the yellow sheer ribbon, make a shoestring bow chain tying 15 bows approximately 4" (10cm) apart.

make satin bow

Cut 7 yards (6m) of the moss green satin ribbon. Make a bow with eight loops that are as wide as the pillow. Staple in place as you create the loops.

add streamers

Cut three moss green ribbon streamers measuring 24" (61cm), 36" (91cm) and 48" (122cm) in length. With the bow upside down, staple the center of each streamer into the center of the bow. Make sure the shiny sides of the streamers are facing toward the bow. Position each streamer in a different direction. You will have a total of six trailing streamers in all.

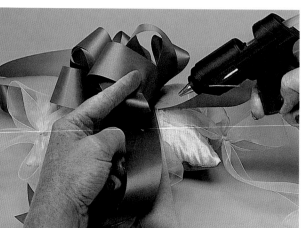

glue satin bow

Using a hot glue gun, glue the moss green satin bow with streamers to the center of the pillow.

add yellow bows

Cut the sheer ribbon bow chain into three streamers with five bows on each. With a hot glue gun, glue one end of each streamer to the pillow under the moss green bow.

add hydrangea and gerbera daisy

Glue the purple hydrangea blossom to the center of the bow. Cut the stem from the gerbera daisy and glue it onto the hydrangea.

add freesia

Glue the two stems of freesia behind the gerbera daisy and into the hydrangea blossom in opposite directions.

add ribbon for rings

Cut a piece of yellow sheer ribbon measuring 24" (61cm) in length. Feed the ribbon through the front two loops. The rings will be tied onto the pillow with this ribbon.

✦

TO SAVE TIME, prepare the ribbon and pillow well in advance and add the flowers the day of your wedding. ✦

BASKET *and* HALO

Your flower girl will be delighted to walk down the aisle carrying

this adorable basket decorated with spray roses, heather and lisianthus.

And with the halo to match, she will surely look like a little angel.

fresh flowers

- 8 STEMS OF MINUETTE SPRAY ROSES
- 6 STEMS OF PINK LISIANTHUS
- 6 STEMS OF HEATHER
- 1 YARD (91CM) OF SMILAX

supplies

- WHITE PRINCESS BASKET
- 1/2" (13MM) DIAMETER HALO FORM
- SILK WHITE ROSE PETALS
- 5' (2M) OF 7/8" (22MM) SHEER WHITE RIBBON
- 5' (2M) OF 1/4" (0.6CM) HOT PINK DOUBLE-FACED SATIN RIBBON
- 5' (2M) OF 5/8" (16MM) WHITE PICOT RIBBON
- WHITE CHENILLE STEMS
- 1/4" (6MM) WIDE WATERPROOF TAPE
- HOT GLUE GUN
- WIRE CUTTERS

basket

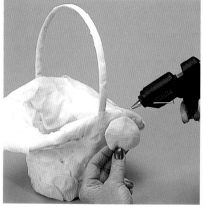

add rose petals

Using the hot glue gun, glue and completely cover the basket inside and out with the silk white rose petals.

attach smilax

Use three short chenille stems to secure the smilax to the basket handle by tightly twisting the stems around the top and sides of the handle.

create nosegay

Cut the buds off of two stems of minuette spray roses, leaving 3" (8cm) stems on each. Cut one stem of heather into four sprigs. Holding the roses in your hand to form a tight nosegay, insert the sprigs of heather randomly. Secure with waterproof tape.

attach bouquet to basket

Trim all three ribbons to measure 5' (2m) in length. Layer them one on top of another and make six loops approximately 2" (5cm) long. Start the loops near the center of the ribbon. Twist a chenille stem tightly around the center of the bow. Attach the bow to the nosegay by twisting the chenille stem around the bow and the nosegay. Secure the nosegay to the end of the basket handle by twisting the ends around the handle. Trim excess with wire cutters. Repeat on other side.

✦

FILL THIS adorable basket with rose petals so your flower girl can leave a pretty trail as she walks down the aisle.

✦

halo

make bow

Trim the three ribbons to measure 5' (1.5m) in length. Layer them one on top of another. Make a bow with six 2" (5cm) loops. Start the loops near the center of the ribbon strands. The remaining ribbons will hang down like streamers. Twist a chenille stem around the center of the bow to secure.

attach bow

Attach the bow to the halo form by twisting the ends of the chenille stem tightly around the form to secure it.

add lisianthus and heather

Use a hot glue gun to glue lisianthus blossoms around the halo form. Next, snip five stems of heather into several 1" (3cm) sprigs. In a scalloped pattern, glue the heather sprigs around the top and bottom of the halo form among the lisianthus blossoms.

add minuette spray roses

Cut the rose blossoms from their stems, leaving only a slight stem on each. Glue the roses randomly onto the halo. Eighteen rose blossoms were used for this project.

✦

YOUR FLOWER GIRL will look like an angel sent from heaven while wearing this gorgeous halo of fresh flowers. Keep this headpiece in a cool place, and store in a container, safe from over-excited little hands! ✦

POMANDER *with* HALO *and* SASH

This matching set includes an easy-to-carry pomander, a sash and a halo. The delphinium, freesia and roses in varying hues of purple and blue blend together for a stunning combination.

fresh flowers

- 3 STEMS OF LIGHT BLUE DELPHINIUM
- 7 STEMS OF DARK BLUE DELPHINIUM
- 20-25 STEMS OF LAVENDER FREESIA (FOR VARIATION)
- 12 LAVENDER ROSES

supplies

- 4" (10CM) WET FOAM BALL
- 2MM CRIMP BEADS
- 6MM PURPLE BEADS
- #5 STRAIGHT BLUE IRIS BUGLE BEADS
- 18" (46CM) OF 1½" (4CM) WIDE IVORY DOUBLE SATIN RIBBON
- 18" (46CM) OF $^{3}/_{16}$" (5MM) WIDE LAVENDER PICOT SATIN RIBBON
- DRINKING STRAW
- FLORAL WIRE
- 24-GAUGE VINYL-COATED BEAD WIRE
- 3" (8CM) WIRED WOODEN FLORAL PICKS
- ½" (13MM) GREEN WATERPROOF TAPE
- SPRAY ADHESIVE
- FLORAL ADHESIVE
- HOT GLUE GUN
- PLIERS

pomander

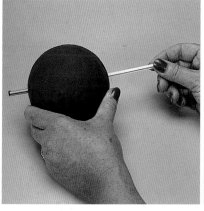
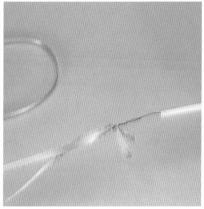
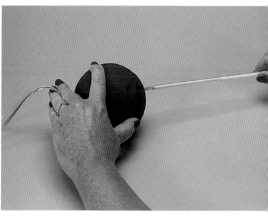

prepare foam ball

Submerge the foam ball in water for ten minutes. Insert a straw through the center of the ball. Do not pull the straw completely through. Leave the straw in the ball.

insert ribbon into straw

Attach the ends of the $3/16$" (0.5cm) lavender ribbon to the floral wire and insert it into the straw.

remove straw

Leaving the ribbon in the desired position for length, remove the straw from the ball. Be sure to hold the ribbon on the other side so it does not slip out of the foam ball. Cut the ribbon ends from the wire and leave the streamers hanging.

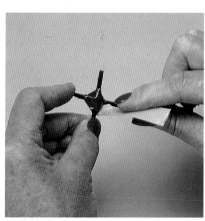
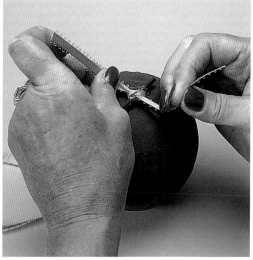

attach ribbon anchor

To hold the ribbon in place, tie a square knot around the ribbon anchor with the ribbon ends. This becomes the bottom of the pomander and will prevent the ribbon from sliding through the ball.

make ribbon anchor

Cut two wooden floral picks to $2\frac{1}{2}$" (6cm) each. Form an X. Wrap the X in place tightly with waterproof tape.

add delphinium

Cut several sprigs from each stem of delphinium. Cut the stems to 2" (5cm) in length. Insert the dark blue delphinium sprigs, completely covering the ball. Insert the light blue delphinium sprigs randomly throughout the pomander. For easy arranging, hang the pomander on a hanger over a door.

insert roses

Cut 12 lavender roses with 1" (3cm) stems. Insert them randomly throughout the pomander. Be sure to insert the flowers at a consistent depth to maintain the ball's shape.

make beading

Start with a crimp bead at the end of the bead wire. Randomly add purple and blue beads onto the vinyl-coated bead wire. Make two strands of beads, one each, measuring 8½" (22cm) and 9½" (24cm) long. Finish each strand with a crimp bead. Fold each strand in half and wrap the wire from a wooden floral pick around the center of the strands. Twist tightly onto the pick to hold. Insert the pick into the bottom center of the pomander.

◆ THIS POMANDER can be made a few days in advance if it is kept in a cool place. To store until the big day, hang it on a doorknob or coat hanger to avoid any flat spots. Other small flowers can be used for this project as well. ◆

halo and sash

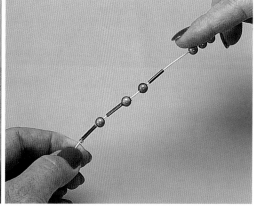

begin beading

Make a beaded strand long enough to be wrapped twice as a halo with trailers. To determine length, have the flower girl present to measure the diameter of the top of her head and the desired length. Start with a crimp bead at the end of the bead wire. Pinch the crimp bead on the end of the strand with pliers.

add beads

Randomly add the purple and blue iris bugle beads.

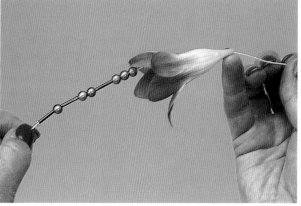

trim freesia blossoms

Clip the individual blossoms from the freesia stems.

add freesia blossoms

Randomly thread the lavender freesia blossoms onto the vinyl-coated bead wire between beaded sections. Each strand should finish with a bead.

make halo

Wrap the beaded strands together to make the halo. The free ends become the trailers.

twist to secure

At the base of the halo, twist the strands around each other to secure.

create sash

Cut the 1½" (4cm) wide ivory ribbon to approximately 18" (46cm) in length. Determine the length of the sash by the size of the flower girl's waist and whether it will be tied in the back with a bow. Start with a crimp bead at the end of the bead wire. Randomly add the purple beads, blue iris bugle beads and lavender freesia blossoms onto the vinyl-coated bead wire. When adding the freesia blossoms onto the strand, remove the individual blossom from the freesia stem and thread onto the bead wire. Make one strand of beads measuring slightly less than the diameter of the flower girl's waist. Finish the strand with a crimp bead.

REFRIGERATE THE HALO in a small storage box. Be careful not to tangle flowing strands of the halo.

Give this sash your own personal flair by using different bead colors and styles. You can also substitute the flowers for daisies, delphinium blossoms, stephanotis or even silk flowers for a keepsake. ✦

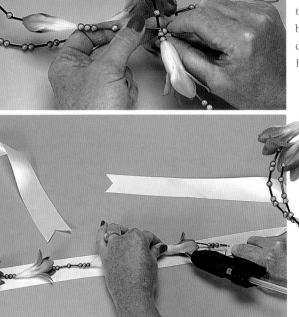

flowers for the CEREMONY *and* RECEPTION

Whether in a church, a hall, your home or any other venue you choose, your wedding ceremony and reception decorations should reflect the overall style of the wedding. The first thing to consider when selecting your flowers is the space itself. Is there enough room for large floral arrangements, or would smaller bunches of flowers look more appealing? Is it a lavish setting, where large, extravagant arrangements are appropriate, or is it a quaint setting that will be better suited for understated arrangements?

To get the most out of your wedding budget, place flower arrangements where guests focus most of their attention. A beautiful altar arrangement at the ceremony or a colorful cake topper and base for the cake table at the reception may be better suited for your wedding than several small arrangements placed throughout the location.

The floral theme of your special day should carry over from the ceremony to the reception. One way to do this is to use your bridal and bridesmaids' bouquets as floral decorations for the head table. When choosing table decorations, opt for centerpieces that don't obstruct the view and conversation of your guests. After all, you want them to enjoy the festivities as much as you will!

CANDLE

The unity candle is a symbol of two lives becoming one.

Adorned with tangerine roses, blue delphinium and peach

tulips, this is a glowing representation of the commitment

shared between the bride and groom.

fresh flowers

+ 10-15 STEMS OF LIGHT BLUE DELPHINIUM
+ 30 TANGERINE SPRAY ROSES
+ 10-15 PEACH FRENCH TULIPS
+ 10 STEMS OF CAMELLIA FOLIAGE
+ 10-15 STEMS OF RUSCUS FOLIAGE

supplies

+ 12" (30CM) WET FLORAL FOAM RING
+ TWO 12" (30CM) WHITE TAPER CANDLES
+ ONE 3" X 12" (8CM X 30CM) WHITE PILLAR CANDLE
+ LEAF SHINE
+ HOT GLUE GUN

prepare foam ring

Submerge the floral foam ring in water for ten minutes. Mark an X where the taper candles will be inserted into the foam. Cut sprigs of camellia foliage from the stems measuring 3" to 6" (8cm to 15cm) in length. Each sprig should have a 1" (3cm) stem for insertion into the foam. Cover the foam ring evenly with the sprigs. Leave a spot for the candles at the X marks. Spray the ring with leaf shine.

insert candles and add ruscus

Insert the candles into the ring. Cut sprigs of ruscus from the stem measuring 3" to 6" (8cm to 15cm) in length. Insert these sprigs randomly throughout the floral ring. Spray with leaf shine.

add spray roses

Using three to four stems of tangerine spray roses, trim the blossoms to have 3" (8cm) stems. Insert the roses randomly throughout the floral ring.

add tulips

Cut the French tulips to have 4" (10cm) stems. Insert them randomly throughout the floral ring at various heights.

add delphinium

Trim sprigs from light blue delphinium stems measuring 3" to 6" (8cm to 15cm) in length. Insert the delphinium sprigs randomly throughout the floral ring. This will add a soft contrast of color to the other flowers.

decorate pillar candle

Snip the rose blossoms from the remaining stems of spray roses at the base. Remove all green leaves from the roses. Using a hot glue gun, glue the rose heads onto the pillar candle. Cover the candle, but leave the wick exposed. Glue the rose blossoms at an angle and in clusters for depth and ease in covering.

TO HYDRATE the candle ring, place it in a low pan filled with water. It can be arranged a few days in advance if kept in the refrigerator or in a cool, dark place. The tulips are likely to grow while in the arrangement, so you may need to trim the stems before the big event.

t u l i p

PEW DECORATION

The flowers that decorate the wedding site are nearly as important as the ceremony itself. After all, they are the first things your guests will see when they arrive. These white and blue flowers, tucked into a shimmering white cone, will set the mood for love.

fresh flowers

- ✦ 4 WHITE TULIPS
- ✦ 3 STEMS OF BLUE DELPHINIUM

supplies

- ✦ 8½" X 11" (22CM X 28CM) SHIMMERING WHITE VELLUM PAPER
- ✦ 7 YARDS (6M) OF ⅝ " (16MM) WIDE WISTERIA BLUE DOUBLE-FACED SATIN RIBBON
- ✦ ½" (13MM) WHITE WATERPROOF TAPE
- ✦ SPRAY ADHESIVE
- ✦ HOT GLUE GUN
- ✦ CRAFT KNIFE

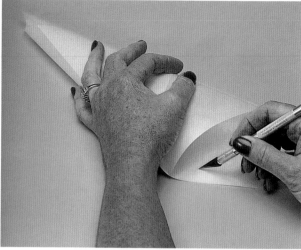

create cone

Roll vellum paper into a cone at an angle. One corner should stick up from the top back part of the cone. To secure the vellum, spray a small amount of spray adhesive onto the inside of the back flap that is wrapped around the front of the cone.

cut slits in cone

Using a craft knife, cut two slits measuring approximately 5/8" (16mm) in length into the inside upper part of the cone tip. Place these slits on opposite sides of the cone.

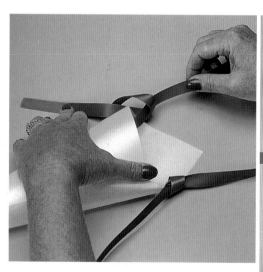

attach bows

Make three bows using the wisteria blue satin ribbon. Spacing the bows evenly down the front of the cone, glue each bow to the cone using a hot glue gun.

make handle

Evenly thread 40" (102cm) of the wisteria blue satin ribbon through the slits to make a handle for hanging the cone. Knot the ribbon ends, leaving 6" (15cm) streamers on each side.

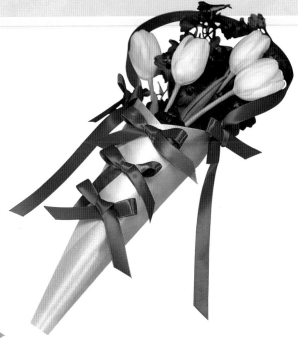

arrange flowers

Arrange four white tulips and three blue delphinium stems in your hand, positioning the delphinium and one tulip taller than the other three tulips. Flowers should look like they are sprouting from the cone. Wrap the stems with waterproof tape to secure.

✦ THIS BOUQUET CAN be made up to three days in advance if it is held in a vase and kept in a cool place. If any buds should open before your special day, be sure to remove the stamens from the center of the flowers. They will stain clothing and hands easily. ✦

alstroemeria PEW DECORATION

fresh flowers

+ 3 WHITE ALSTROEMERIA

+ 4 PINK ROSES

supplies

+ 5" (13CM) WIDE WHITE DOUBLE-FACED SATIN RIBBON

+ WHITE CHENILLE STEM

+ GREEN WATERPROOF TAPE

1. prepare flower cluster

Arrange the alstroemeria and roses in your hand. Cut the stems to the desired length and wrap with waterproof tape.

2. make bow and add flowers

Starting in the center of the ribbon, make a bow with six loops measuring 6" to 10" (15cm to 25cm). Twist a chenille stem around the center of the bow. The remaining ribbons become streamers. Add the flower cluster and tightly twist the chenille stem around it to secure.

lavender

CANDLE
CENTERPIECE

Light up the room with more than just your smile on that special day.

The soft pastels of the lavender tulips and pink spray roses will make

every table at your wedding reception feel warm and inviting.

fresh flowers

- 10 LAVENDER TULIPS
- 3 STEMS OF BABY'S BREATH
- 5 PINK SPRAY ROSES
- 1 BUNCH OF PITTOSPORUM

supplies

- 60 TO 65 YARDS (55M TO 59M) OF 1½" (4CM) WIDE LAVENDER SHEER SATIN WIRED RIBBON
- ½" (13MM) GREEN WATERPROOF FLORAL TAPE
- 1 SHEET OF 22" X 30" (56CM X 76CM) LAVENDER MULBERRY PAPER
- FIVE 3" (8CM) ROUND PILLAR CANDLES, 5" (13CM), 8" (20CM) AND 11" (28CM) IN HEIGHT
- CRAFT KNIFE

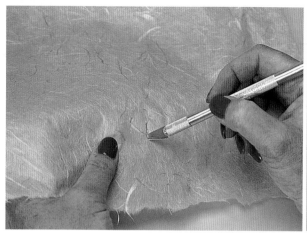

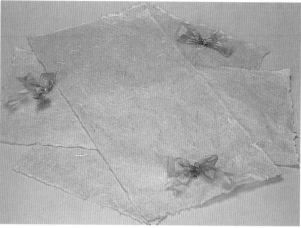

prepare mulberry paper

Cut the mulberry paper into three equal pieces. The sheets should measure approximately 22" x 10" (56cm x 25cm) each. Feather the edges. At one end of each piece of mulberry paper, centered and about 2" (5cm) in, use a craft knife to cut two slits about ½" (13mm) apart and wide enough for the ribbon to slide through.

make bows and arrange paper

Cut a piece of ribbon measuring 18" (46cm) in length. Slide the ribbon under and through the slit in the mulberry paper. Tie the ribbon into a shoestring bow. Repeat this step on the other two ribbon ends. Place the sheets of mulberry paper diagonally in the center of the table, alternating the placement of the bows. This becomes the place mat for your centerpiece.

arrange nosegay

Trim ten lavender tulips to have 6" (15cm) stems and 12 sprigs of pittosporum to have 4" (10.2cm) stems. In your hand, cluster the tulips together at varied heights. Surround the tulips with the sprigs of pittosporum, making sure that their placement is slightly lower. Make a tight nosegay.

wrap nosegay

Secure the nosegay by wrapping the stems tightly with waterproof floral tape.

add ribbon

Cut a piece of ribbon measuring 18" (46cm) in length. Wrap the ribbon around the nosegay stems and tie it into a square knot to secure it. Make additional nosegays with pink spray roses, pittosporum and baby's breath. Wrap and tie them with ribbon as you did for the tulip nosegay.

tie candles with ribbon

Trim five pieces of ribbon measuring 15" to 18" (38cm to 46cm) in length. Wrap the pieces of ribbon around the top third of each candle and tie it with a square knot to secure it. Trim the ribbon ends with an angled cut for a more finished appearance.

◆

THE CANDLES AND MULBERRY PAPER in this simple and elegant centerpiece can be prepared well in advance. Be sure to store the mulberry paper flat and store the candles in a cool place to keep them from melting. ◆

fruit and flowers

CENTERPIECE

Who says fruit is just for eating? Fresh apples and grapes are

paired with hydrangeas, roses and Queen Anne's lace for a wedding

centerpiece that has never looked—or tasted—so delicious!

fresh flowers

+ 7 GALA APPLES
+ 5 BUNCHES OF GREEN GRAPES
+ 3 LARGE GREEN HYDRANGEAS
+ 36 LIGHT PINK ROSES
+ 4 STEMS OF QUEEN ANNE'S LACE

supplies

+ 8" (20CM) DIAMETER WEATHERED
  MOSS CONTAINER
+ 1 BRICK WET FLORAL FOAM
+ FLORAL WIRE
+ SEVEN 12" (30CM) SKEWERS
+ 12" (30CM) WIRED WOODEN FLORAL PICKS
+ 1/4" (6MM) WIDE GREEN WATERPROOF
  FLORAL TAPE

prepare floral foam

Submerge two-thirds of a brick of floral foam in water for ten minutes. Criss-cross waterproof tape, securing the foam into a weathered moss container. If the container is covered in an oily film that is keeping the tape from adhering, wipe it with a paper towel.

add hydrangeas

Trim three green hydrangeas with 4" to 5" (10cm to 13cm) stems. Insert around the perimeter of the container.

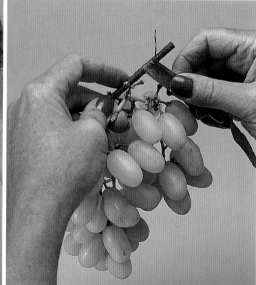

add apples

Cut seven skewers to measure 6" to 8" (15cm to 20cm) in length. Insert the skewers at different angles into the apples. Randomly insert the apples into the foam and around the hydrangea blossoms, going from one side of the arrangement to the other.

wire and secure grapes

Wire five bunches of green grapes onto wooden floral picks. Secure the grapes onto the wire and wooden pick with floral tape, pulling and stretching tightly as you go.

add grapes

Insert three bunches of grapes around the base of the arrangement. Trim the wooden picks to the desired lengths. Insert the remaining two bunches off-center and in the top portion.

add roses and queen anne's lace

Insert 36 light pink roses at varied heights. Next, trim sprigs of Queen Anne's lace with 4" (10cm) stems and insert them randomly throughout the centerpiece.

✦
TO ENSURE that the apples and grapes stay fresh, this arrangement should be made no more than a day in advance. Keep the centerpiece in a cool, dry place (and away from your hungry wedding party!). ✦

BASKET-WEAVE CENTERPIECE

Add sunshine to your reception with this cheerful centerpiece.

In this arrangement, which also doubles as a flower vase, flax foliage

and lily grass are woven around a colorful sunflower. Simply stunning!

fresh flowers

+ 1 LARGE SUNFLOWER OR SEVERAL
  SMALL SUNFLOWERS

+ 8-12 BLADES OF FLAX FOLIAGE

+ 1 BUNCH OF LILY GRASS

supplies

+ 7½" (19CM) TALL ROUND GLASS VASE,
  3" (8CM) IN DIAMETER

+ 2 RUBBER BANDS

+ SPRAY ADHESIVE

+ FLORAL ADHESIVE

+ WATERPROOF FLORAL TAPE

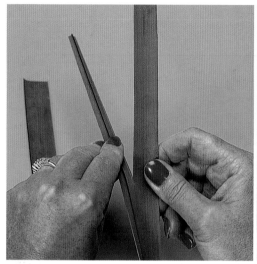

trim flax

Cut the heavy ends of the flax leaves off and tear the leaves in half. The flatter the leaves, the easier they are to work with.

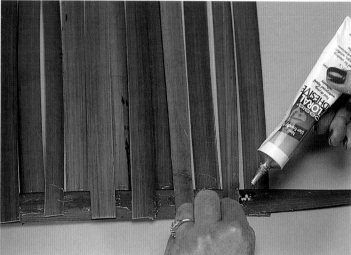

assemble flax foliage leaves

Assemble the flax leaves, approximately 11" (28cm) in length, into parallel rows. The width of the parallel rows should be that of the diameter of the vase. Weave another flax leaf in and out of the parallel rows. Secure this row using floral adhesive where each blade of flax meets. Trim the horizontal leaf ends that are sticking out to be even with the parallel row.

continue weaving

Weave additional flax leaves. Construct this woven pattern or mat to the height of your vase, in this case 7" (18cm).

secure flax

Secure the side and top blades of flax with floral adhesive. Trim the sides. Do not trim the top—they should remain free and loose.

5. add lily grass

Slightly trim the blunt ends of the lily grass. Place two rubber bands around the glass vase and insert the lily grass blades under the bands. Arrange the blunt ends first at the bottom of the vase. Completely cover the vase and hold the grass in place with waterproof floral tape at the top and base. Cut the rubber bands loose.

6. secure woven mat

Using spray adhesive, glue the woven mat of flax leaves around the grass-covered vase. Spray the back of the mat and the outside grasses of the vase where the mat will be secured. Wrap with rubber bands and set aside for a few hours. Remove the bands when dry.

7. add sunflower

Cut the sunflower stem to a length that allows the flower to extend past the tips of the grasses. Add water to the vase and insert the sunflower. Trim the tips of the flax blades at an angle with staggering heights. Add more sunflowers if desired for a fuller look.

✦ PREPARE THIS CENTERPIECE a few days in advance and store in a cool place. Mist the arrangements occasionally with water to keep the sunflowers from drying out and the grass from curling. ✦

rose

TOPIARY

Bring your wedding reception to life with this lavish topiary

of asiatic lilies, gerbera daisies and roses. The delicate shades

of peach and yellow will accent a variety of color schemes.

fresh flowers

- 10-15 PEACH ASIATIC LILIES
- 6 PEACH GERBERA DAISIES
- 25 YELLOW ROSES
- 10 PEACH SPRAY ROSES

supplies

- 4" (10CM) DIAMETER WET FOAM BALL
- TALL CANDLESTICK FOR A 3" (8CM) PILLAR CANDLE
- FLORAL ADHESIVE

attach foam ball

Secure the wet foam ball to the top of the candlestick. Apply more adhesive if necessary.

apply glue

Submerge the floral ball in water for ten minutes. Apply floral adhesive to the rim of the candlestick where the foam ball will be placed.

trim asiatic lilies

Trim the open lily blossoms off, leaving 2" to 3" (5cm to 8cm) stems on each blossom.

add asiatic lilies

Randomly insert the lily stems into the foam, completely covering the ball.

add gerbera daisies

Randomly insert the gerbera daisies with 3" (8cm) stems throughout the centerpiece.

add yellow roses

Trim the roses to have 3" (8cm) stems. Randomly insert the roses throughout the centerpiece.

add peach spray roses

Trim the stems of the spray roses to measure 3" (8cm) in length. Fill in the gaps throughout the centerpiece.

◆ PURCHASE LILIES that are open, or get them a few days before you need them so that the lily blossoms can open fully. ✦

tulip

TABLE WREATH

The right table decorations can enhance the atmosphere

of your wedding reception. This lovely floral centerpiece will

impress the guests at your reception without distracting them

from the real center of attention—the happy couple!

fresh flowers

+ 16 WHITE TULIPS
+ 3 WHITE CALLA LILIES
+ 10-15 STEMS OF SEEDED EUCALYPTUS

supplies

+ 15" (38CM) WET FLORAL FOAM RING
+ FLORAL ADHESIVE
+ LEAF SHINE

insert seeded eucalyptus

Submerge the floral foam ring in water for ten minutes. Cut sprigs of seeded eucalyptus measuring 3" to 7" (8cm to 18cm) in length. Insert the sprigs throughout the ring and cover it completely. Spray it with leaf shine. When inserting the flowers, move the eucalyptus leaves aside to avoid blocking the foam.

add calla lilies

Trim three white calla lilies to have stems measuring 4" (10cm), 10" (25cm) and 12" (30cm). Insert the stems of the calla lilies into the inside center of the ring at varied heights.

add tulips

Trim five white tulips, two with 5" (13cm) stems, two with 6" (15cm) stems and one with an 11" (28cm) stem. Insert into the inside center of the floral ring along with the calla lilies.

add hanging tulips

Trim seven tulips, three with 7" (18cm) stems, two with 9" (23cm) stems and two with 11" (28cm) stems. Insert these tulips into the lower part of the floral ring under the calla lilies, slightly off to the left. Place them so they hang from the wreath.

connect tulips

Trim four tulips to have 4" (10cm) stems. Insert the tulips into the face of the wreath, connecting the upper tulips with the hanging tulips.

✦ CUT THE TULIP STEMS slightly shorter than you would like them, as they will grow a bit before your reception. Mist the flowers lightly every day with water, and keep the arrangements out of direct sunlight, which will speed up the growth of tulips. Trim the stems as necessary. ✦

TOPPER *and* BASE

Your fairy tale wedding won't be complete without this bright
and beautiful wedding cake topper and base. The contrast of the
snow white cake and the rich red, magenta and lavender flowers
make this arrangement almost too beautiful to eat!

fresh flowers

- 3 MINIATURE PLUM CALLA LILIES
- 12-15 STEMS OF RED COCKSCOMB
- 12-15 STEMS OF MAGENTA COCKSCOMB
- 37 OPEN RED ROSES
- 23 LAVENDER ROSES
- 1 STEM OF MING FERN
- 1 STEM OF BOXWOOD
- 1 BUNCH OF BEAR GRASS

supplies

- 1 WET FLORAL FOAM CAGE
- 14" (36CM) STYROFOAM RING
- LEAF SHINE
- HOT GLUE GUN

cake topper

add ming fern

Submerge the floral foam cage in water for ten minutes. Cut 3" (8cm) sprigs of ming fern from the stem and insert evenly throughout the cage. Completely cover and spray with leaf shine.

add boxwood

Cut off 3" to 6" (8cm to 15cm) sprigs of boxwood from the stem and insert them randomly throughout the arrangement. Spray with leaf shine.

insert miniature calla lilies

Trim three stems of miniature calla lilies to measure 3" (8cm), 4" (10cm) and 6" (15cm) in length. Insert the stems in the center of the cage at different heights and in a triangular pattern. They should be trumpeting out of the top of the cake.

add roses and cockscomb

Trim the stems of the roses to measure 1" to 2" (3cm to 5cm) in length. Insert an open red rose in the top, slightly off center. This will become the front of the arrangement. Insert the three lavender roses around the floral cage. Next, trim the stem of the cockscomb to measure 3" (8cm) in length. Insert randomly around the sides of the cage.

add bear grass

Add the desired amount of bear grass measuring 12" to 18" (30cm to 46cm) in length into the top of the cage. Curl some of the ends with scissors.

cake base

add cockscomb
Randomly cover the sides of the foam ring with the magenta and red cockscomb. Secure with a hot glue gun.

add lavender roses
Trim the lavender roses to have 2" to 3" (5cm to 8cm) stems. Randomly insert the lavender roses into the foam among the cockscomb and secure with a hot glue gun.

add red roses
Trim the stems of the roses to measure 2" to 3" (5cm to 8cm) in length. Insert randomly throughout the sides of the foam ring. Add the remaining cockscomb to fill in bare spots and secure with hot glue.

◆ PURCHASE YOUR ROSES approximately five days before your wedding. This is because it takes at least three days for red roses to be fully opened. Trim the stems daily and place the roses in water to open them before adding them to the cake. ◆

resources

DOMESTIC RESOURCES

MARIEMONT FLORIST, INC.
7257 Wooster Pike
Cincinnati, OH 45227
(800) 437-3567
www.mariemontflorist.com
✦ Contact author, general information and assistance

C.M. OFFRAY & SON, INC.
360 Route 24
Chester, NJ 07930
(800) 551-LION
www.offray.com
✦ Decorative ribbons

DESIGN MASTER COLOR TOOL INC.
P.O. Box 601
Boulder, CO 80306
(303) 443-5214
www.dmcolor.com
✦ Floral color sprays, paints and tints

FLORACRAFT
One Longfellow Place
P.O. Box 400
Ludington, MI 49431
(616) 845-0240
www.floracraft.com
✦ Floral sheet foam and general floral supplies

FLORIST DIRECTORY
www.eflorist.com
✦ Web directory to assist in finding a florist in
your area

SAVE-ON-CRAFTS
1660 N. 25th Ave. Suite 101
Phoenix, AZ 85023
(602) 993-3364
fax (602)993-3285
www.save-on-crafts.com
✦ Floral wires, foam, adhesives, tapes, raffia, moss,
silk flowers, greenery, ivy garlands and topiary forms

SOCIETY OF AMERICAN FLORISTS
1601 Duke St.
Alexandria, VA 22314
(800) 336-4743
www.safnow.org
✦ General information about the floral industry

W.J. COWEE, INC.
28 Taylor Ave.
P.O. Box 248
Berlin, NY 12022
(800) 658-2233
www.cowee.com
✦ Wooden floral picks and general floral supplies

INTERNATIONAL RESOURCES

FLORAL ART MALL
21/262 Centerway Rd.
Orewa
New Zealand
www.floralartmall.com
+64 9427 5681
✦ Retailer of fresh and silk flowers, florist supplies
and books.

index

Personalize your wedding
with elegant handmade accessories and decor!

Beautiful Bridal Accessories You Can Make

Jacquelynne Johnson

Here's a smart, sophisticated alternative to store-bought wedding accessories. Jacquelynne Johnson shows you how to make an incredible variety of elegant adornments for the bride, wedding party, friends and family. Personalized to fit your style, each of these 22 step-by-step projects is inexpensive and easy to make with simple embellishing techniques and a glue gun.

ISBN 1-55870-624-0, paperback, 128 pages, #70570-K

Creative Wedding Florals You Can Make

Terry L. Rye

Create your very own floral arrangements for priceless wedding memories with a personal touch. Terry Rye will teach you step by step how to design more than 20 stunning designs. You'll find something for every part of the wedding—from bouquets and boutonnieres to pew decorations, table centerpieces and wedding cake toppers.

ISBN 1-55870-560-0, paperback, 128 pages, #70488-K

Creative Wedding Keepsakes You Can Make

Terry L. Rye and Laurel Tudor

Make your wedding elegant and unforgettable with these beautiful keepsake ideas. From the bridal veil to the guest book, this book provides 21 step-by-step projects that are fun, affordable and surprisingly easy to make. Best of all, each project is made from non-perishable materials, so everything can be finished well in advance of the big day.

ISBN 1-55870-559-7, paperback, 128 pages, #70487-K

Memory Makers Wedding Idea Book

Memory Makers Books

This unique guide combines dazzling layout ideas with easy-to-follow instructions for creating a gorgeous wedding scrapbook album. You'll find layouts for every event, including the engagement, shower, wedding ceremony, reception, honeymoon and more. Every aspect of the scrapbooking process is covered, from organizing photos and selecting an album to choosing a visual theme and writing journal entries.

ISBN 1-892127-08-3, paperback, 128 pages, #31788-K

These titles are available from your local art and craft retailer, bookseller, online supplier or by calling 1-800-448-0915.